Happy Birthday, AMERICA!

by Natalie Goldstein

PEARSON

Scott Foresman

Editorial Offices: Glenview, Illinois • Parsippany, New Jersey • New York, New York
Sales Offices: Needham, Massachusetts • Duluth, Georgia • Glenview, Illinois
Coppell, Texas • Sacramento, California • Mesa, Arizona

This is the Declaration of Independence.
It gave Americans **freedom**.

The Declaration of Independence

Thomas Jefferson helped write the Declaration.
It was approved on July 4, 1776.

Thomas Jefferson

George Washington was our first **President**.

George Washington

In 1777 Independence Day was celebrated.

Cannons were fired on July 4, 1777.

On July 4 fireworks shoot up into the sky.

Americans watch fireworks on the
Fourth of July.

Many **citizens** have parades.

People have parades on the Fourth of July.

Glossary

citizen a member of a state and country

freedom a person's right to make choices

President our country's leader